BABY SIGNING

With

ROLLO BEAR

British Version

BABY SIGNING

With

ROLLO BEAR

British Version

Early Communication for Ages 3 months to 5 years

Picture Dictionary with over 200 signs!

By Kiddisign

Books to Publish, October 2010

1st Edition – First published in Great Britain 2010 by Books to Publish

A cataloguing record of this book is available from the Library and Archives UK

Printed and bound in the US or the UK
By Lightningsource Ltd.

ISBN (13): 978-0-9567346-0-0

CONTENTS

Foreword

Welcome to Baby Signing with Rollo Bear!

Vonnie LaVelle of Kiddisign's Baby Signing with Rollo Bear, is an experienced Baby Signer, a Certified Presenter with Sign2Me™ in America and holds a British Sign Language Qualification.

Kiddisign started Baby Signing with Parent and Baby/Toddler classes in 2004 and then taught in Nurseries from 2006. Through the experiences with teaching, they realised there was a need for a new resource to help everyone learn Baby Signing at their own pace and they compiled their first book in 2008.

This new edition, a picture dictionary, introduces 'Rollo the Teaching Bear' who gives a fun approach to signing for babies and young infants. Rollo Bear also signs the alphabet, days of the week and numbers in this edition, to give a basic knowledge of signing to any age group.

Kiddisign had extensive media attention in the UK, Ireland and America in 2009. They highlighted the use of sign language to assist children of any age to show their feelings and to convey what they were experiencing around them.

Introduction

The baby signing concept came from an interpreter called Joseph Garcia. He realised that hearing babies and toddlers were copying his signs and then parents noticed the babies were signing when they wished their needs to be met or to convey that they needed their nappy changed!

The research of over 20 years has shown that babies who sign when they are young are less frustrated and therefore cry less, have accelerated verbal language development, and also show more positive interest in books. They can clearly communicate specific thoughts and understand questions or be able to give answers before speech has formed!

Baby Signing can be integrated into a baby and toddlers' daily routine very easily by starting with simple food signs. Very young babies have been known to sign but the most effective age for a baby learning signs is from 5 months old. There is no age limit to learning sign language, and the older a child is, the quicker they imitate the sign and make the connection to the word and action. Speech and signs are communicated together, so the child will create a 'mind-word-picture' situation in their minds and their speech will be accelerated rather than delayed.

Once a child has begun talking, they may still want to use signs if they are struggling with a new word, for fun to accompany nursery rhymes, or to communicate with younger siblings.

Research

The research completed on Baby Signing started in 1987 by Joseph Garcia, who studied the effects on babies at Alaska Pacific University. This research showed that signing eases frustration, helps babies to communicate and that signs are picked up easily at around 6 months or so. In 2009, Mr. Garcia commented at a conference that Kiddisign attended, that new research is showing signs are communicated from 0 months onwards!

Between 1987 and 2009, Dr. Linda Acredolo and Dr. Susan Goodwin, University of California at Davis, studied signing with small babies through to 8 years of age. They now have over 20 years of research papers, showing that in babies who sign, there is greater verbal language development, higher IQ's, a baby will share it's world more, eases frustration and increases parent-child bond.

In 2007, Dr. Gwyneth Doherty-Sneddon, Stirling University in Scotland, found that it helped very small children to communicate, eased child and parent frustration and helped toddlers develop socially acceptable behaviour.

Other studies continue and new research is showing that older babies are able to sign the alphabet! It is amazing that sign language can be added into a child's life on a daily basis which aids their development.

How to Start Signing

1. Use lots of repetition and over emphasise the signing procedure. Your child may only use the 'sign' when they really need something, so be patient. A younger child of, say, 5 months old, could take a few weeks to sign back.

2. Make eye contact while you sign and say the word.

3. Sign the word, before, during and after an action, always in the context of the action i.e. when giving food, sign 'eat' first, then food, then sign and word again.

4. 'More' can be used as, more food, more play, more park, more milk, etc…

5. Comment and sign when your baby is looking at you or something in particular e.g. Duck in the bath or pond, Aeroplane, Food, Toys.

6. You can use a teddy bear to teach the signs for pain, etc. e.g. Teddy hurts his head and it's sore – show the sign for 'pain'. Babies teething will tend to hold their mouth while they're teething – this is an excellent opportunity to teach 'pain'.

7. The sign for 'medicine' is used before, during and after giving the child medicine. The baby learns that communicating this way quickly relieves them of pain. Some people find the sign for 'medicine' controversial but a young baby or small child does not understand the concept of mis-using this sign. They are more interested in being helped.

8. ……..(cont.)

8.   The sign for 'hot' can be used firstly via food – show them the sign and say the food is too 'hot'. Your child will then connect to this sign and be able to interpret it when they are feeling too 'hot' or you can use this method with 'cold' too!

9.   If you see your child using a part-sign, then reiterate the sign again until they can form the full sign. They may still continue to use the simplified sign, which is fine – as long as your family understands what your child is communicating to them.

10. Emphasise the key sign and word during a sentence.

11. Dialect in sign language is similar as in speech. Therefore, you may come across various versions of some of the signs. This is fine as you are the one communicating with your baby. Most of the everyday signs you will find are generally the same across the UK.

12. The whole family and carers should join in with the signing but give them the simple, necessary signs to begin with!

Please download our FREE practice sheets on our website at www.kiddisign.com!

THE ALPHABET

A

index
finger
points to
thumb

B

C

D

E

F

index finger points to index finger

G

H

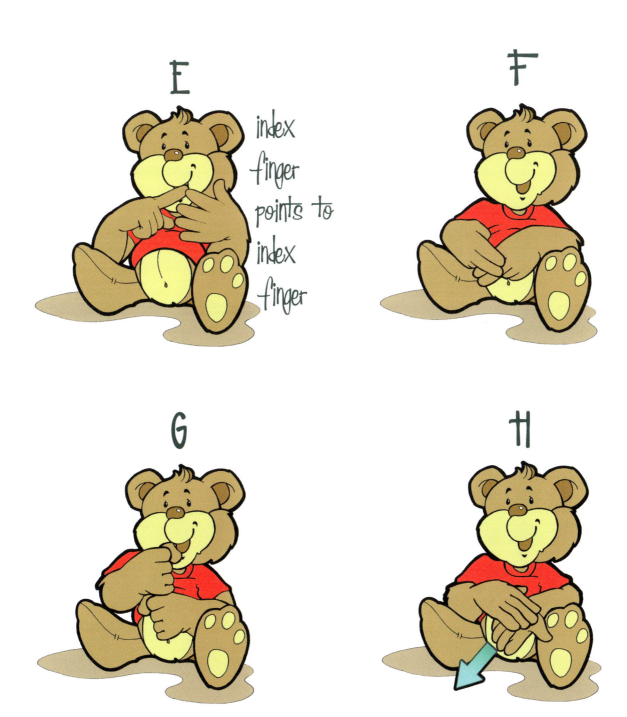

I

index
finger
points to
middle
finger

J

move index
finger down
middle finger
& along
palm

K

L

M

N

O

index
finger
points to
ring finger

P

Q

index finger
goes through
other thumb
& index
fingers

R

S

two pinkie
fingers
crossed

T

U

V

W

X

index finger points to pinkie finger

y

z

index finger
follows
arrow down

NUMBERS

One

Two

this sign can be used two fingers together

Three

Four

Five

Six

Seven

Eight

Nine

Ten

DAYS OF THE WEEK

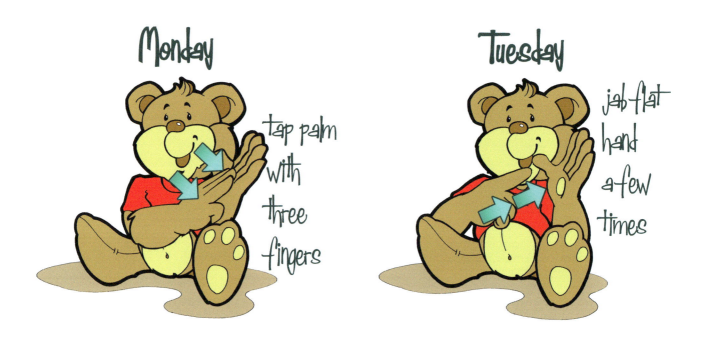

Monday — tap palm with three fingers

Tuesday — jab flat hand a few times

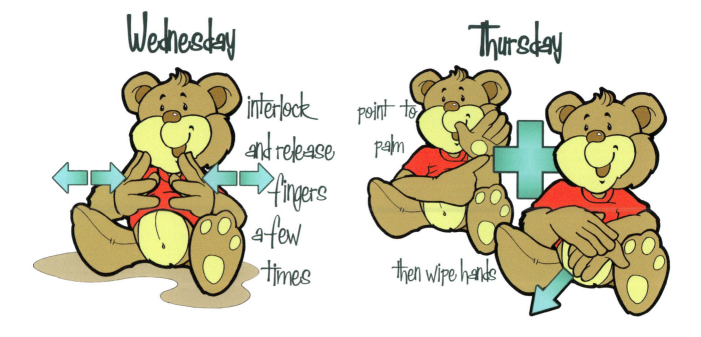

Wednesday — interlock and release fingers a few times

Thursday — point to palm then wipe hands

Friday

move two fingers on both hands in flat circles

(or some people tap the fingers)

Saturday

point to tip of fingers then to palm

Sunday

pat flat hands together

ANIMALS

Bird

move two fingers like beak

Butterfly

link thumbs & fan hands then flap

Cat

Chicken

use thumb & forefinger to pick off other hand

Cow

tap head several times

Crocodile

open & close hands & arms like big jaws

Dog

Donkey

Duck

like a beak movement

Elephant

start with hand cupped by face then move down & out

Farm

move thumb downwards

Fish

tilt hand side to side in a forward motion

Fly

move hand like fly buzzing around

Frog

move cupped hand in & out from neck

Giraffe

hand at base of neck moving upwards

Goat

Guinea Pig

put fist on top of each other

then sign for pig

Hamster

clawed hands swivel on cheeks

Hippo

open & close clenched fists

Horse

move both hands together up & down

Lion

bring clawed hand over head from ear to ear

Monkey

scratch under armpits

Mouse

point into side of nose

Owl

Pig

Sheep

move pinkies round in circles

Spider

move hand along like spider walking

Squirrel

move hand out in big sweep from hip

Tiger

spread fingers & pull hands apart

Turkey

flap elbows like birds wings

Zebra

drag clawed hand across body a few times

COLOURS

Black

Blue

rub skin in circles

Brown

clasp fingers together & pull down

Gold

put fist on top of each other

& then explode hands out

Green

move top hand around in semi circles

Orange

claw hand across mouth

Pink

move finger down lips

Purple

fingers then jump away open

Red

flick bottom lip

Silver

cross pinkie fingers

& then explode hands out

White

flick middle finger

Yellow

slide index finger in direction of arrow

A - Z

DICTIONARY

Aeroplane

extend thumb & little-finger & move hand around

Angry

scrape chest upwards

Apple

open mouth pretending to eat apple & crunch

Baby

Bad

Ball

make the shape of a ball with your hands

Banana

pretend to peel a banana

Biscuit

tap elbow of other arm

Boat

fingertips together move hands forward in a wavy motion

Book

open thumbs & hands out like a book

Bread

slice top hand over flat hand back & forth

Brother / Running

fists move up & down

Brush Teeth

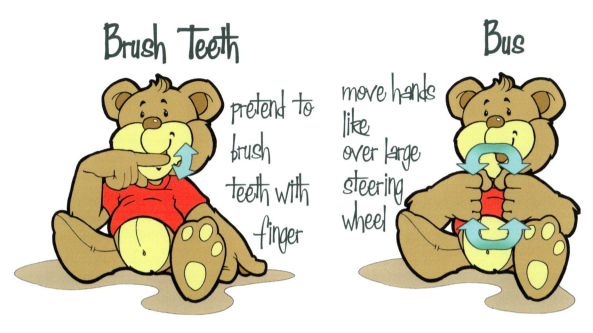

pretend to brush teeth with finger

Bus

move hands like over large steering wheel

Cake

claw hand repeatedly

Car

smaller steering wheel hands

Catch

pretend to catch a ball & close hand to fist

Chair / Sat / Sit

move both hands downwards

Change / Nappy

continually change fists

Clean

wipe palm motion

Coat / Jacket

pretend to put on coat

Cold / Chills

shake top body, arms & fists as if cold

Cook

pretend to hold a spoon stirring a bowl

Cup

pretend to hold dainty cup & tip hand towards face

Daddy

two taps

Dance

make 'V' shape with fingers & wave around

Dark / Night

cross arms in front

Dirty

clench fists & rub wrists together in small circles

Don't Touch / No

tap two fingers on back of hand & shake head

Drink / Water

tip hand towards mouth

Dry

sweep thumb across fingers

Eat

move clawed hand towards mouth

Fall

top hand falls into bottom palm

Family

move two fingers on both hands in flat circles

Flower

mime smelling a flower passing hand under nose

Fork

show fingers like prongs on a fork

Friend

shake your own hand

Full / Full Up

bring flat hand up from chest to under chin

Gentle

stroke top hand towards you

Get Dressed / Clothes

brush hands & move arms down

Girl

index
finger
brushes
cheek

Good

closed
hand &
thumb
raised

Grand ma

put fist
on top
of each
other

then place three
fingers on palm

Grand pa

put fist
on top
of each
other

then place two
fingers on back of two fingers

Happy

slap top hand over bottom hand towards you

Hat

pull down imaginary hat on head

Hear / Listen / Noise

cup hand to your ear

Help

move two hands in & up

Home / House

Hot

move
clawed hand
quickly away
from mouth

Hug

Hungry

semi
circle
tummy

I Love You

hug & then point

Ice Cream

pretend to lick ice cream cone

Ill / Unwell

with little fingers extended. drag hands down chest

Jump

fingers jump onto hand

Lamp / Light

Light

start with arms horizontal & cross them upwards

Look / See

move two fingers of one hand away from your eyes

Market / Shop

Medicine

little finger of one hand rotates in open 'O' of other hand

Men / Man

move hand together & down

Milk

open hand and squeeze as shown

More

two taps

Mummy

two taps

Music

act like a conductor

No / Stop

move hand forward then stop

None / All gone

move flat hands up & out

Out

Pain

shake hands up & down

Park / Garden

tap chest twice with horizontal flat hand

Play

wiggle fingers & move hands in circles upwards

Queen / King / Crown

tap head with open hand

Rain

wiggle fingers on way down

Rainbow

move hand in big rainbow motion

Sad

Sand

rub thumb & fingers whilst raising hands

Scared / Frightened

hold chest

Sea

make a wavy motion

Shoes

move cupped hand up other hand

Signing

hands move in opposite circles

Sister

bring finger down nose

Skip

fingers flick over flat hand

Slide

slide a hand down in a straight line

Snow

flutter fingers & zigzag hands down

Sore Gums

point to gums then shake hands up & down

Sore Head

point to head then shake hands up & down

Sore Throat

point to throat then shake hands up & down

Sorry

move fist in a circle around chest

Spoon

pretend to spoon-food up towards mouth

Sun / Sunshine

Swimming

like a breast stroke movement

Swing

swing arms outwards & backwards

Teddy Bear

scrunch chest with fingers

Telephone

mime a telephone

Television

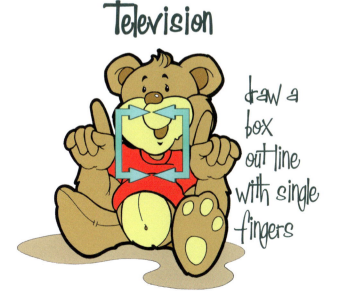

draw a box outline with single fingers

Thank You

fingers to mouth then move hand forward

Tired / Sleep

Today

move hands slightley up & down to reinforce sign

Toilet

tap index finger on outside edge of other hand

Tomorrow

pull hand away from face with bent finger

Towel

pretend to use towel to dry behind neck

Toys

move both index fingers in same direction circles

Train

arm by side at a right angle, move shoulder & arm in circular motion

Tree

shake hand like leaves on a tree

Twinkle / Star

wiggle fingers up in air

Up

Want

sweep flat hand away from chest

Wet

open & close fingers a few times

What

When

drum cheek with fingers

Where

move flat hands in opposite circles

Which

Who

Why

tap chest a few times

Wind

blow with your mouth & sweep your hands to the side

Woman / Lady

fingers
brush
cheek

INDEX

INDEX

Lightning Source UK Ltd.
Milton Keynes UK
UKIC03n0635260915
259307UK00010B/52

9780956734600